OTHER HELEN EXLEY BOOKS IN THIS SERIES:
A Portfolio of Business Jokes
A Round of Golf Jokes
A Triumph of over 50s' Jokes
A Romp of Naughty Jokes
A Spread of over 40s' Jokes

Published simultaneously in 2006 by Helen Exley Giftbooks
in Great Britain, and Helen Exley Giftbooks LLC in the USA.

Cartoons © Bill Stott 2006
Selection and arrangement © Helen Exley 2006
The moral right of the author has been asserted.

Printed in China

ISBN 1-84634-080-2

12 11 10 9 8 7 6 5 4 3 2 1

The publishers gratefully acknowledge permission to reprint copyright material. They
would be pleased to hear from any copyright holders not here acknowledged.
**Important copyright notice: Philip Brooke, Pam Brown, Susan Curzon, Jenny
De Souza, Peter Dugdale, Mike Knowles, Stuart and Linda Macfarlane, Jon
Newbold, Alex Stanger, Adrian Tydd, Angus Walker © Helen Exley 2006**

**Helen Exley Giftbooks Ltd, 16 Chalk Hill, Watford,
Herts WD19 4BG, UK
Helen Exley Giftbooks LLC, 185 Main Street,
Spencer, MA 01562, USA
www.helenexleygiftbooks.com**

Over the Hill

CARTOONS BY BILL STOTT

A HELEN EXLEY GIFTBOOK

The best thing
about being over the hill
is that now
you can have some fun
and free-wheel
down the other side.

ESTHER REES

So, what is old?

Age is a question of mind over matter.
If you don't mind it doesn't matter.

DAN INGHAM

Old age is always fifteen years older than I am.

BERNARD M. BARUCH

Age is something that doesn't matter,
unless you are a cheese.

BILLIE BURKE

Growing old is more like a habit which a
busy man has no time to form.

ANDRÉ MAUROIS

Over 30? It has its advantages

You can now afford
all the things you no longer want.

You no longer blush when you chat up
members of the opposite sex –
because you no longer chat up
members of the opposite sex.

For the first time you are able to count
all the hairs on your head.

When watching TV
you can irritate others by telling them
the endings to all those old films
you saw the first time round.

You can eat as much as you wish
and blame the consequences
on middle-age spread.

STUART AND LINDA MACFARLANE

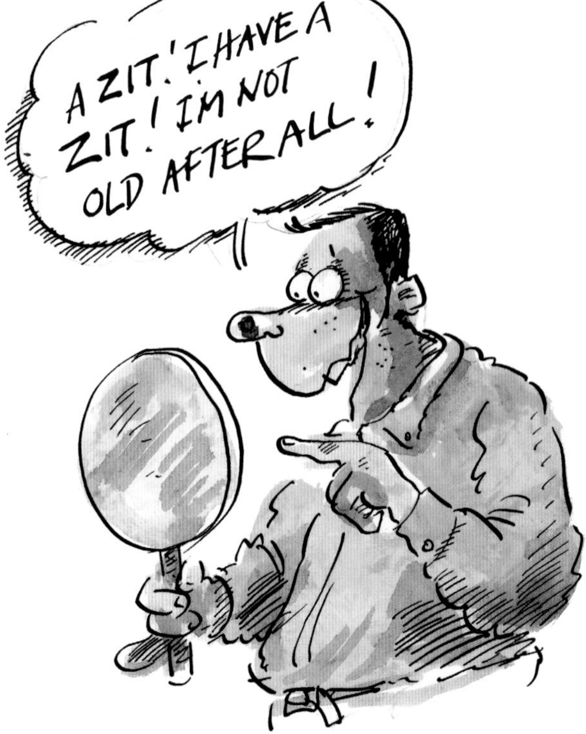
A ZIT! I HAVE A ZIT! I'M NOT OLD AFTER ALL!

Now I'm over 50
my doctor says I should go out
and get more fresh air and exercise.
I said "All right,
I'll drive with the car
windows open."

ANGUS WALKER

I'm getting to an age
when I can only enjoy
the last sport left.
It is called hunting your spectacles.

LORD GREY OF FALLODEN

Except for the occasional heart attack,
I feel as young as I ever did.

ROBERT BENCHLEY

18TH TEE

It's something you grow into

Anyone can get old.
All you have to do is live long enough.

GROUCHO MARX

I do not call myself really old yet.
Not till a young woman offers me
her seat in a railway compartment
will that tragedy really be mine.

E. V. LUCAS

When in his seventies Sir Malcolm Sargent
was asked to what he attributed his great age,
he said, "I suppose I must attribute it
to the fact that I haven't died yet."

AUTHOR UNKNOWN

"Don't worry about it – you don't look a day over 50.
Mind you, you always were a mature 50."

"Mirror, mirror... don't ask!"

Who is the fairest?

As your body begins to sag
and wilt there are three stages
in keeping your ego intact:

1.

Trying to convince yourself
that you look young.

2.

Trying to fool your friends
that you look young.

3.

Trying to describe to the plastic surgeon
the miracle that you would like them
to perform to make you look young.

STUART AND LINDA MACFARLANE

You're a piece of ancient history

You know you must be pretty ancient
when your grandchildren
ask you for your personal recollections
of Queen Victoria
and life before electricity.

PETER DUGDALE

"Hi grandad..."

Those tell-tale signs...

There are three ways to tell if you're getting on: people of your own age start looking older than you: you become convinced you're suddenly equipped with a snooze button: and you start getting symptoms in the places you used to get urges.

DENIS NORDEN

Middle age is...

...when you're faced with two temptations
and you choose the one that will get you
home by 9 o'clock.

RONALD REAGAN

...when comfort triumphs
at last over fashion.

PAM BROWN

...when your clothes no longer fit,
and it's you who needs the alterations.

EARL WILSON

You know you're getting old
when you stoop to tie your shoes
and wonder what else you can do
while you're down there.

GEORGE BURNS

Birthday blues

Just think, if only you could snap your fingers
on the birthday you wanted
and never grow any older!
HUH Birthdays won't even let you
do that because you've got that much arthritis
your fingers won't snap.

SUSAN CURZON, AGE 12

Age – something to brag about in your
wine-cellar and forget in a birthday book.

FROM "10,000 JOKES, TOASTS AND STORIES"

When you have a birthday
and you are middle aged
your friends all clink their glasses
and cheer and it gives you a headache.

PHILIP BROOKE, AGE 8

"He just keeps muttering, it's all downhill from here...."

I'm at the age where food
has taken the place
of sex in my life.
In fact,
I've just had a mirror
put over my kitchen table.

RODNEY DANGERFIELD

In middle age it's helpful to remember
a few basic diet rules:

1.
If no one sees you eat it, it has no calories.

2.
If you eat snacks quickly,
or with your head in the fridge,
they have no calories.

3.
If you drink diet cola
with a chocolate bar
they cancel each other out.

N.J.R.

"Okay – you're the same weight as you were at 35.
You were a chubby 35."

"They wouldn't serve me – said I didn't look old enough you'll have to go."

The secret of Staying young

A woman walked up to a little old man
rocking in a chair on his porch.
"I couldn't help noticing how happy you look,"
she said. "What's your secret
for a long, happy life?"

"I smoke three packets of cigarettes a day,"
he said. "I also drink a case of whiskey
a week, eat fatty foods,
and never exercise."

"That's amazing," the woman said.
"How old are you?"
"Twenty-six," he said.

JOE CLARO,
FROM "THE RANDOM HOUSE BOOK
OF JOKES AND ANECDOTES"

Three stages of recession:

Hairdo
Hairdid
Hairdone

DAVID E. BESWICK,
FROM "BALD MEN ALWAYS COME OUT ON TOP"

It's so ironic. The human race
has the technology to travel to the moon.
But we have failed miserably
in developing a wig that can't be detected
by a short-sighted moron from
the other side of a darkened room.

STUART AND LINDA MACFARLANE

"Receding hairline? Nonsense –
I've <u>always</u> combed my hair forward."

The memory's the first to go...

"Gerry's always been very fussy about his appearance... pity about his memory."

Joe arrived home from a shopping trip
to the supermarket.
As his wife checked through the groceries
she complained that
he had forgotten many of the items
he was supposed to buy.
"At least I remembered to drive home
in the car this time,"
announced Joe with an air of satisfaction.
"Car! What car?
We don't own a car!" shrieked his wife.

STUART AND LINDA MACFARLANE

Mel Brooks' secrets of longevity

1.

Don't run for a bus –
there'll always be another.

2.

Never, ever touch fried food.

3.

Stay out of a Ferrari
or any other small Italian car.

4.

Eat fruit – a nectarine –
or even a rotten plum is good.

MEL BROOKS

"You found a wrinkle? Give it 25 years
and you won't have to look for them."

I have reached the age
when I look just as good standing on my head
as I do right side up.

FRANK SULLIVAN

I wouldn't say my face
was getting more wrinkled,
but the other day it took
a bead of sweat two hours
to reach my chin.

MIKE KNOWLES

She was 102.
She didn't have wrinkles.
She had pleats....

DENNIS WOLFBERG

Desperately seeking

THE FIVE STAGES OF THIRTY-SOMETHING COURTSHIP

1.
Look for a willing partner.

2.
Search relentlessly
for a willing partner.

3.
Hunt desperately
for a willing partner.

4.
Engage FBI's help
in searching for
a willing partner.

5.
Abandon hope
of ever finding
a willing partner.

It's hard to believe
that in our early twenties
we were so choosy
about the people we dated!
Did they have their own car?
Did they have zits?
Did they wear
fashionable clothes?
One small imperfection
and they were told
to get lost.
Now, if anyone
accidentally collides
with our cart
in the supermarket,
we pester them for
their phone number.

STUART AND LINDA MACFARLANE

Older and wiser

The older I grow
the more I distrust the familiar doctrine
that age brings wisdom.

H. L. MENCKEN

By the time you get to fifty, people
expect you to be mature,
responsible, wise and dignified.
This is the time to disillusion them.

PETER DUGDALE

I was telling my son about the advantages
of being over 50. "As you get older," I said,
"you get wiser." He looked at me and replied
"In that case you must be a genius."

ANGUS WALKER

"Why can't you be boring and out of touch
like other kids' dads?"

Spare parts!

I'm going to the garage
for my 10,000 mile service,"
said Robert to his wife.
"Don't you mean you're taking the car
for its service?"
quizzed his wife.
"No, I've got so many spare parts
I think it's better to be checked by a garage
than a doctor."

STUART AND LINDA MACFARLANE

An old man gives good advice
in order to console himself
for no longer being able to set
a bad example.

LA ROCHEFOUCAULD

Lola's husband Joseph, a merchant,
was asked why he subscribed to Playboy magazine.
"I read Playboy for the same reason
that I read National Geographic,
so's I can see all the sights
I'm too danged old to visit."

FROM "A TREASURY OF SENIOR HUMOR"

At my age, by the time I find temptation,
I'm too tired to give into it.

E.C. MCKENZIE,
FROM "14,000 QUIPS AND QUOTES
FOR WRITERS AND SPEAKERS"

Young men want to be faithful and are not,
old men want to be faithless and cannot.

OSCAR WILDE

The dreaded birthday

"Are you going to have candles
on your birthday cake?"
"No, it's a birthday party,
not a torchlight procession."

CINDY PATTERSON

You know you're getting old when the candles
cost more than the cake.

BOB HOPE

My wife's best friend has just celebrated
the twentieth anniversary
of her twenty-ninth birthday.

KEVIN GOLDSTEIN-JACKSON, FROM "JOKES FOR TELLING"

It was my girlfriend's birthday
last Wednesday – when I asked her
how old she was she said "pushing thirty"
but slapped my face
when I asked her from which direction.

AUTHOR UNKNOWN

"I wonder what you'd look like without your chins?"

"HMMM."

when it all starts to sag...

You can only hold your stomach in
for so many years.

BURT REYNOLDS

You know you're getting on
when your bottom hits the settee
before you've even sat down,
and the supermarket cart
rattles less than your dentures.

JON NEWBOLD

It's hard to feel as fit as a fiddle
when you're shaped like a cello.

B. L.

The over thirties' glossary

LOVE:

A transient state of mind when logic
and reason are abandoned.
Condition is temporary.
Occurs less frequently with age.
Men often confuse it with lust.

SEX:

An act most frequently performed alone.
When performed with a partner
it is purely for their pleasure
as you would rather be sleeping
or watching television.
Anticipation always better
than the act..

YOUTH:
A far off mystical land populated
by undeserving idiots.
There are no roads leading
IN to this land, only OUT of it.

AMBITION:
A burning desire for the status quo
to continue for as long as possible.

MIDDLE AGE:
A blasphemous expression.

STUART AND LINDA MACFARLANE

"Quick sing something – I'm losing my rhythm!"

Laid back lovemaking

Take a more laid back approach to lovemaking.
Here are some positions to try:

The Tête-à-Tête:
In this position the couple lie side by side
and simultaneously complain of headaches.

The Zzzz:
Action postponed until morning.

The Snatch:
A ten minute cuddle while the baby sleeps.

The Chiller:
After ten minutes a break is taken
to have an ice cream.

The Frenzy:
This position requires some movement
and should only be undertaken
after a full medical check up.

STUART AND LINDA MACFARLANE

Middle age:
when you begin to
exchange your emotions
for symptoms.

IRVIN COBB

The disadvantage of being old
is not looking as nice
as you did when you were young.
It is like looking in
a before and after picture
but the other way round.

GINO MIELE

who wants to live forever?

Life's a tough proposition but the first
hundred years are the hardest.

WILSON MIZNER

Youth is a disease from which we all recover.

DOROTHY FULDHEIM

Longevity is one of the more
dubious rewards of virtue.

NGAIO MARSH

I'll tell ya how to stay young:
Hang around with older people.

BOB HOPE

"Yes, yes, a good body for a man of 60, but
you're only here to have your bunions treated..."

Staying in shape!

You have to stay in shape.
My grandmother, she started walking
five miles a day when she was 60.
She's 97 today and we don't know
where the hell she is.

ELLEN DEGENERES

When you're my age,
you go out to the beach
and turn a wonderful colour.
Blue.
It's from holding in your stomach.

ROBERT ORBEN,
FROM "2100 LAUGHS FOR ALL OCCASIONS"

Oldies' maxim on youth:

Youth is expert in everything and experienced in nothing.

STUART AND LINDA MACFARLANE

"The advantage of great age, huge wealth and complete ownership is that you can say anything you like, you boring young idiot."

"You know you're over the hill when your most-loved movies
are shown at 11 o'clock in the morning."

Signs that you're an old wreck

Your birth certificate is written in roman numerals.

Archaeologists dig up things you remember
from your childhood.

You remember a time when you could fix
the television by giving it a good thump.

Your best-loved music is only available
on vinyl.

Even wonderbras can't give you a lift.

You become aware that the print size in books
and magazines has started to get smaller.

You don't have too much trouble bending down –
it's getting up again that's the problem.

STUART AND LINDA MACFARLANE

Don't call me "old"

The day I give in and allow the word
bifocal to enter my vocabulary,
is the day I'll also stop dying my roots,
having my teeth capped
and cantilevering my boobs.
It'll be a courageous moment
and fortunately I shall
be too dead to see it.
"Glasses to glasses and
bust to bust...."

MAUREEN LIPMAN,
FROM "YOU CAN READ ME LIKE A BOOK"

"Now that's what a grandma should look like, Grandma."

Downhill all the way...

I'm at an age where my back goes
out more than I do.

PHYLLIS DILLER

You know you're getting older
when you wake up
with that morning after feeling
and you didn't do anything
the night before.

S.L.P.

When you've reached a certain age
and think that a face-lift
or a trendy way of dressing
will make you feel twenty years younger,
remember – nothing can fool
a flight of stairs.

DENIS NORDEN

"He was a beautiful child…
unfortunately he peaked at twelve."

"60? Amazing, that's wonderful –
I had you at least 70 –
we were at the same school – remember?"

You can't believe a woman...

One should never trust a woman
who tells one her real age.
A woman who would tell one that,
would tell one anything.

OSCAR WILDE

My wife never lies about her age.
She just tells everyone she's as old as I am.
Then she lies about my age.

J.K.N.

Man is old when he begins
to hide his age;
woman, when she begins to tell hers.

OSCAR WILDE

Sex

Past thirty? You are now in your prime.
The opposite sex will find you irresistible.
So put on your cardigan, slacks and slippers
and prepare to be hunted.

STUART AND LINDA MACFARLANE

"Look there he goes... thirty-one
and bought his first pack of viagra!"

Consolation for baldness

What's the advantage of hair, anyhow?
It blows in your eyes
And it flops on your brow,
Disguising the shape of your scholarly head;
It often is grey and it sometimes is red.
Perhaps it is golden and ringleted, but
It needs to be combed and it has to be cut,
And even at best it is nothing to boast of.
Because it's what barbarous men
Have the most of;
Then challenge your mirror, defiant
And careless.
For lots of our handsome people
Are hairless.

ARTHUR GUTTERMAN

God created a few perfect heads; the rest he covered with hair.

DAVID BESWICK

Too old for exercise

The only reason
I would take up jogging is so I could hear
heavy breathing again.

ERMA BOMBECK

You know you've reached middle age
when your weightlifting
consists merely of standing up.

BOB HOPE

I'm not into working out.
My philosophy: No pain, no pain.

CAROL LEIFER

"You've got a keep fit attitude problem."

"I'm actually older than my husband."

Putting a brave face on it

Two fraternity brothers
were attending their class reunion,
the first time they'd seen one another for thirty years.
One asked, "Is your wife still as pretty
as she was when we were all in school together?"
"Yeah, she is…
but it takes her an hour longer."

FROM "A TREASURY OF SENIOR HUMOR"

When you reach sixty your beautician
sends you this letter.
It says, "Dear Customer, I can no longer help you.
From this day on you're on your own."

MICHELE KOLFF

Seduction lines for geriatrics

Excuse me, were you smiling at me
or have you just forgotten your false teeth?

When I look at you my pacemaker
starts thumping.

If I put my teeth in will you give me a snog?

That's a sexy red dress you're wearing.
I can almost see your ankles.

I love your wig.
Is it made from genuine rat hair?

Are you dancing or are you just feeling
a bit wobbly?

STUART AND LINDA MACFARLANE

"Hey baby! Love the way you move!"

Respect your elders

The best part of being an oldie
is that you get to be eccentric and
young people have to be polite and
patronize your idiosyncrasies.

NIELA ELIASON

From the earlier times the old have rubbed
it into the young that they are wiser than they,
and before the young had discovered
what nonsense this was they were too old,
and it profited them to
carry on the imposture.

WILLIAM SOMERSET MAUGHAM

"He bet his allowance that he could do more press-ups than Grandad. He lost."

Falling apart...

You have arrived at old age when
all you can put your teeth into is a glass.

E. C. MCKENZIE

I know a fella
who had one of those hair transplants
and it was kind of touching.
He bought a comb and asked
if it came with instructions!

ROBERT ORBEN,
FROM "2100 LAUGHS FOR ALL OCCASIONS"

When you are old your body creaks
and your knees knock and your teeth fall out.

ADRIAN TYDD, AGE 10

"Hairpiece, dentures, bifocals —
there's not a great deal of me left, is there."

How to blow
your life savings

- Have a set of diamond-studded
  false teeth made – even if
  you have all your own teeth.

- Bury them and create a puzzle
  so your relatives can spend years
  hunting for them.

- Have a walking frame crafted
  from gold.

STUART AND LINDA MACFARLANE

"I'd like it souped-up."

A second honeymoon

A couple in their sixties
are on their second honeymoon,
reminiscing about the good old days
when they were newly-weds.
Full of nostalgia,
the wife says, "Do you recall
how you used to nibble on my ear lobes?"
"Yes," replies her husband.
"Well why don't you do it anymore?"
"Because by the time I've put my teeth in,
the urge has gone!"

JENNY DE SOUZA

"Don't worry about it – it happens quite often
on our second honeymoon breaks...."

The bald truth

The probability of your toupee
falling off is directly proportional
to the attractiveness of the person
you are trying to impress.

Ninety-nine percent of toupees
are discarded in disgust and humiliation
within a month of purchase.
Rather than throw yours away,
recycle it as a mop,
a bird's nest or a winter jacket
for a Chihuahua.

STUART AND LINDA MACFARLANE

"Bald spot!? What do you mean, bald spot?"

"For a fifty year old, you're in terrible shape."

"Nonsense. I demand a second opinion."

"Ok you're ugly too."

One of the saddest things of
growing old is that you might have
an illness that cannot be cured
and the doctor might say.
"We are very sorry, very, very,
but we are going to have
to put you down."

ALEX STANGER, AGE 7

The great Battle of the Bulge

DIET:
A method of reducing food intake
without eating less.
Always performed at a future date –
usually tomorrow.

The two invariable laws of dieting:

1.

The harder and longer you diet
the greater your weight gain will be.

2.

For every kilo your best friend loses
you will gain two.

STUART AND LINDA MACFARLANE

"Prepare to meet thy doom!"

Ancient

When I was young, the Dead Sea was still alive.

GEORGE BURNS

You know you're ancient
when you can remember a time
when errors were blamed on human beings
rather than computers.

NICOLE REUBEN

He's so old his blood type
was discontinued.

BILL DANA

She was so old when she went to school
they didn't have history.

RODNEY DANGERFIELD

"I'll be 10 tomorrow Aunt Doreen –
were you ever 10?"

I don't feel old, just downright worn out.

WILL SMITH, AGE 110

Age seldom arrives smoothly or quickly.
It's more often a succession of jerks.

JEAN RHYS

Old age is when most of the names
in your little black book are doctors.

E. C. MCKENZIE,
FROM "14,000 QUIPS AND QUOTES
FOR WRITERS AND SPEAKERS"

I smoke cigars because of my age –
if I don't have something to hang onto
I might fall down.

GEORGE BURNS

"You know what they say about being as old as you feel?
I think I'm about 328."

Old wrecks' quiz

DETERMINE HOW OLD YOU REALLY ARE!

1. How attractive are you to the opposite sex?
a) I have a constant stream of admirers.
b) A secret admirer once sent me a card.
c) People turn away as I walk down the street.

**2. When you see your body in the mirror
   what do you think?**
a) I'm living proof that youth can be eternal.
b) I look good for a ninety-year-old.
   It's a pity that I'm only sixty-three.
c) Help! I've turned into a dinosaur.

3. How good is your memory?
a) I can remember the day I was born.
b) I can remember all the days of the week.
c) I have only a vague recollection of starting this qui

Allocate 3 points for As, 2 points for Bs and
1 point for Cs.

TOTALS:

3-5 Congratulations on reaching the ripe old age of 200.

6-7 You may think you are old but you are really young at heart.

8-9 You have all the attractiveness and attributes of a youngster. Are you sure you are an oldie?

STUART AND LINDA MACFARLANE

At 50 you still get "the urge" but can't remember what for...

AUTHOR UNKNOWN

Sex after ninety
is like trying to shoot pool with a rope.
Even putting my cigar in its holder is a thrill.

GEORGE BURNS

Sex after sixty:
When relighting your fire means paying
the overdue gas bill.

JON NEWBOLD

My husband never chases another woman.
He's too fine, too decent, too old!

GRACIE ALLEN

"I've never loved anyone so beautiful for so long..."

Eternal youth

The only people who really adore being young are the middle-aged.

PAM BROWN

"Yeah, my dad's on a youth kick too –
every time we meet someone who doesn't know me,
he introduces me as his brother."

Youth is a wonderful thing;
what a crime to waste it on children.

GEORGE BERNARD SHAW

"You have to be impressed. He's 40 today
and he can still get into his flares."

Doomsday

"This is crazy,"
protested Jill to her friend.
"I sympathize with you
about turning thirty next week –
but insisting everyone
wears black to your party
is just ridiculous."

STUART AND LINDA MACFARLANE

"There's no need to feel miserable
on your thirtieth birthday –
there's a whole decade ahead for that."

In the good old days

...Today's antiques were available new.

...You could warm your hands on the radio.

...Knees were shocking.

...Fashion models were not constructed of silicon.

...Old people seemed much older than they do now!

STUART AND LINDA MACFARLANE

That sign of old age:
extolling the past at the expense
of the present.

SYDNEY SMITH

"You just can't get a decent picture these days."

I have everything now
I had twenty years ago –
except now it's all lower.

GYPSY ROSE LEE

Once upon a time I was so beautiful.
My hair was thick and dark and glossy.
My skin was smooth and soft as a ripe peach…
My mouth was dark pink…
My eyes were large and clear…
Unfortunately,
I was four years old at the time.
It's been downhill ever since.

GENEEN ROTH

As a woman grows older,
she starts to suspect that nature is
plotting against her for the benefit of doctors,
dentists, and moisturizer magnates.

NICOLE REUBENS

"When I was 20, getting ready to go out took no time.
Now I'm 40, it takes two hours.
If I ever get to 80, it won't be worth going out."

"That's funny, I could have sworn it was Friday."

At my age
I don't care if my mind starts
to wander – just as long as it
comes back again.

MIKE KNOWLES

I don't let old age bother me.
There are three signs of old age.
Loss of memory...
I forget the other two....

RED SKELTON

You know you're getting older
when you try to straighten out
the wrinkles in your socks
and discover
you're not wearing any.

LEONARD L. KNOT

It's hard to be hip

You know you're out of date when:
You can't name the top ten.

Most of your record collection falls into
the "oldies but goodies" category.

Instead of looking for the action,
you look for peace and quiet.

VICTORIA BLACK, FROM
"MOISTURIZER IS MY RELIGION"

Act your age

Setting a good example for your children
takes all the fun out of middle age.

WILLIAM FEATHER

It's funny how we never get too old
to learn some new ways to be foolish.

E. C. MCKENZIE, FROM
"14,000 QUIPS AND QUOTES FOR WRITERS AND SPEAKERS"

When you're over 50 you can still do
all the things you did when you were 17...
that's if you don't mind making
a complete prat of yourself.

MIKE KNOWLES

"He's into doing things he hasn't done
for a long time. I live in hope."

I am just turning forty
and taking my time about it.

HAROLD LLOYD, AT 77
WHEN ASKED HIS AGE, FROM *THE TIMES*

Life would be infinitely happier
if we could only be born
at the age of eighty and gradually
approach eighteen.

MARK TWAIN

"Yes he is good – just don't ask him how old he is."

No woman should ever
be quite accurate about her age.
It looks so calculating.

OSCAR WILDE

When a woman tells you
her age add on five years
to get her true age.
To be popular, subtract five years
from her actual age
and tell her this is how old she looks.

• • •

Lie detectors have been
used efficiently to convict
murderers, international
jewel thieves and hardened hit men.
However, when attempting
to establish a woman's age
they are woefully inadequate.

STUART AND LINDA MACFARLANE

Baldness: the benefits

1.

There is never any hassle
with dress codes,
flaky dandruff or trying to get
that full-bodied look.

2.

You save countless hours
and dollars at hair salons.

3.

You can use your head
as a reflector when lost at sea.

DAVID E. BESWICK,
FROM "BALD MEN ALWAYS COME OUT ON TOP"

Remember the Teddy Boys?
They used to dab a jar of Brylcreem
on their hair and spend hours
getting the quiff just right.
Now it's a quick rub with some floor polish
and they're off.

MIKE KNOWLES

"I do wish you wouldn't do that."

"No you're not adopted so – yes you will look like me when you are 42."

Kids!

The first half of our lives
is ruined by our parents
and the second half by our children.

CLARENCE DARROW

Middle age is when you stop
criticizing the older generation
and start criticizing
the younger one.

Wrinkles are hereditary.
Parents get them from their children.

DORIS DAY

You know your memory
has started to go when...

...you have déjà vu about events
that happened five minutes ago.

...you keep meeting interesting new people
– in your own home.

...you finally find
what you were looking for, but you
have forgotten why you wanted it.

...you get a big surprise
when you read yesterday's entry
in your diary.

...you forget that you
have a dreadful memory.

STUART AND LINDA MACFARLANE

"He keeps forgetting we had the door moved.
That's the third time he's been through that wall."

The oldest swinger...

The ageing swinger, flattering himself
that he was still a ladies man,
was flirting with a pretty waitress
at his club. "So tell me Darling,
where have you been all my life?"
"Actually, Sir," she smiled,
"for the first forty years of it,
I wasn't even born."

S.L.P.

I may be 50,
but every morning when I get up
I feel like a 20-year-old.
Unfortunately,
there's never one around.

J.K.N.

"Whose is this work of fiction?"

Middle age is when your age
starts to show around the middle....

BOB HOPE

Uses for a gigantic tummy

- Take a job in a department store as an all-year-round Santa.

- Make use of it as a portable shelf.

- Use it to keep the rain off your feet.

- Tattoo flowers on your tummy and enjoy watching them grow as your waistline expands.

- Use it as a bumper when you collide with the furniture.

STUART AND LINDA MACFARLANE

"What do you mean – I look younger
than Carol O'Brien? Carol O"Brien is 56."

When it comes to age, keep them guessing!

I refuse to admit
that I am more than fifty-two,
even if that does
make my sons illegitimate.

NANCY ASTOR

Women are most fascinating between the ages
of thirty-five and forty, after they have won
a few races and know how to pace themselves.
Since few women ever pass forty,
maximum fascination can continue indefinitely.

CHRISTIAN DIOR

As a graduate of the Zsa Zsa Gabor
School of Creative Mathematics,
I honestly do not know how old I am.

ERMA BOMBECK

A medical condition

A middle-aged friend told me
that he had been to
his doctor for a check-up,
after which the doctor
said, "You're in good shape."

"But, Doctor," he protested,
"why do I keep getting
so tired?"

"Youth deficiency," replied the doctor,
"Nothing
but youth deficiency."

LEE AIKMAN

"We've got the test results Mr. Fittock.
Internally you're as fit as a 20-year-old.
Externally, you just <u>look</u> worn out."

An oldie rebellion

I was always taught
to respect my elders and I've now
reached the age when I don't have to
respect anybody.

GEORGE BURNS

Go straight to the front of lines.
If anyone dares to complain, calmly reply,
"Youngsters have got no respect for their
superiors any more."

STUART AND LINDA MACFARLANE

Exercise daily.
Eat wisely.
Die anyway.

AUTHOR UNKNOWN

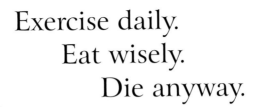

Growing old disgracefully

Sex got me into trouble from the age of fifteen:
I'm hoping that by the time I'm seventy
I'll straighten it out.

HAROLD ROBBINS

Old age doesn't stop men
from chasing women –
it's just they can't remember why.

JENNY DE SOUZA

One should never make one's debut
with a scandal.
One should reserve that to give
an interest to one's old age.

OSCAR WILDE

"So you're 60. So what? A birthday's a birthday!"

Folly forever!

The hair may go.
The teeth may go.
The memory may go.
But the folly goes on forever.

STUART AND LINDA MACFARLANE

Oldies' maxim on life:
Life is for the old to enjoy
and the young to look forward to.

Well done.
You have reached a ripe
old age by good, clean living.
You have refrained from over-indulging
in partying and late nights.
And now?
What the hell – go for it!!!